EQUAL
OPPORTUNITIES
COMMISSION

CW00924299

s

THE GENDER DIVIDE

Performance differences between boys and girls at school

A report from the Office of Her Majesty's Chief Inspector of Schools
and the Equal Opportunities Commission

London: HMSO

ISBN 0 11 350082 3

Office for Standards in Education
Alexandra House
29–33 Kingsway
London WC2B 6SE

Telephone 0171-421 6800

Equal Opportunities Commission
Overseas House
Quay Street
Manchester M3 3HN

Telephone 0161-8339244

Contents

Foreword

This paper, produced jointly by our two organisations, is intended to inform the debate which is currently taking place about education and gender. We hope that it will be useful to a range of people including Registered Inspectors, local education authorities, and schools' senior managements and governing bodies. We recognise that it does not provide the last word on many issues but believe that, firmly grounded in inspection evidence and based on a clear understanding of the legal framework, it offers some key information and poses important questions for schools.

The paper comes at a time when there is a great deal of public interest in the effects of gender on educational achievement. The extent to which boys are under-achieving by comparison with girls is summarised in an early section. We look at some of the issues to do with boys' achievement and make some suggestions for schools to consider.

The issue of boys' achievement must, however, be seen within the context of the overall issue of the provision of equality of opportunity for girls and boys. Girls currently achieve relatively well at age 16, but we have concerns about some aspects of their education too; not least the serious fall-off after 16 in their participation in subjects which could lead to careers in science, engineering and technology. Any national debate about education and gender must take continual account of both sexes in an attempt to ensure not that they achieve equally, but that each has equal opportunity to reach their full potential. Girls and boys need an education which prepares them equally for the challenges and opportunities presented by the changing world of work. The evidence suggests that though some schools demonstrate very good practice others have a considerable way to go.

OFSTED intends to take this area of work forward in several ways. A forthcoming publication on the achievement of young people from ethnic minority groups will comment briefly on the connections between ethnicity and gender as influences on achievement. A review of research findings on education and gender will be produced this year, summarising for teachers the key features of recent research. The new *Framework for Inspection*, in use since April 1996, is likely to bring in more inspection evidence about the performance of girls and boys, and the factors contributing to this, than the previous

Framework and this will inform HMCI's future annual reports. HMI hope to undertake some focused inspections during this year looking in detail at provision for girls and boys.

The Equal Opportunities Commission (EOC) also intends to build on this work. The EOC will use this joint discussion document, with the findings from its research report *Educational Reforms and Gender Equality in Schools*, in its work with national policy makers and local practitioners. The EOC will highlight the key role which gender plays in educational achievement and post-school destinations and encourage equality work as an integral and essential part of improving the quality of education in schools.

The EOC is committed to seeking improved gender equality in education and training and its 1995-99 Corporate Plan identifies development projects in all sectors. In particular, the EOC is encouraging the gender equality element of inspection in schools, colleges, teacher-training and in universities. Alongside this, the EOC wishes to ensure that the expanding nursery education sector meets equality standards which secure the delivery of desirable outcomes for all young girls and boys. The EOC will encourage the development and monitoring of national equality targets through work with key providers, and will inform debate and developments in curriculum, assessment and qualification systems.

This is a discussion document and we would welcome responses from readers. Responses can be sent to the addresses given at the end of the publication.

KAMLESH BAHL
Chairwoman
Equal Opportunities Commission

CHRIS WOODHEAD
Her Majesty's Chief Inspector
Office for Standards in Education

The Legal Framework

- The development of equality of opportunity between the sexes in school owes much to the legal requirements placed on educational establishments by the Sex Discrimination Act 1975 (SDA). This provides a clear legal framework of equal treatment for girls and boys and has produced major changes in the practices of schools, for example, in relation to access to the main curriculum, to curricular options and to extra-curricular activities.

- By putting issues of access and entitlement firmly on the educational agenda, the SDA has also raised the profile and significance of good equal opportunities practice at LEA level and in individual schools. Many schools now have equal opportunity policy statements and are trying to reduce any aspects of their organisation and culture which might treat girls or boys unfairly or inappropriately, and might hinder the educational achievement and personal development of either sex.

- The purpose of the SDA is implicit in later Education Acts, especially in the Education Reform Act 1988 which requires that the curriculum of a maintained school "...promotes the spiritual, moral, cultural, mental and physical development of pupils at the school and of society; and...prepares such pupils for the opportunities, responsibilities and experiences of adult life." Fundamental to this requirement is the notion that this is an equal entitlement for all pupils.

The Implications of the Sex Discrimination Act

- The SDA establishes a pupil's right not to be the victim of sex discrimination, and defines the various forms this might take. It is the duty of the responsible body, usually the governors of the school, to ensure that provision is not discriminatory.

- The SDA requires that applicants for admissions to schools in an area should have access to any school in that area, selective or non-selective, grant maintained or specialist, irrespective of sex. An exception is made for admission to single-sex schools, though their curricular and non-curricular facilities should not be less favourable than those at other schools in the same area. Single-sex schools turning co-educational are subject to the requirements of the SDA regarding admissions and curriculum in co-educational schools. A Transitional Exemption Order can permit discriminatory admissions over a limited period to allow for the phasing in of co-education.

- The SDA requires that all extra-curricular activities such as field trips, clubs, team sports and community work must be equally available to boys and girls and must provide the same standard of opportunities for both sexes. While extra-curricular competitive sports may be offered by associations which are exempted from the SDA because of their voluntary status, where activities are offered by the school equality of access for girls and boys is required.

- Standards of behaviour, restrictions on pupils' dress and appearance, school rules and disciplinary methods must be applied consistently to all pupils regardless of their sex.

- Careers guidance, interviews and literature must be provided on a non discriminatory basis, and visits to employers and opportunities for work experience must be open to all pupils. However, the SDA does allow positive action in vocational education and training to encourage young men and women into non-traditional types of work, such as the establishment of girls-only computer clubs and events to encourage girls contemplating careers in science and engineering.

- The SDA establishes that subjecting pupils to any form of detriment on the grounds of sex is unlawful. For example, schools should not try to balance the numbers of girls and boys in any particular class or stream if this is likely to be detrimental to one sex. Similarly, they should not allocate pupils to mixed age classes on the basis of their sex. However, single-sex classes within mixed schools are lawful provided that the facilities provided to each sex are regarded as equivalent.

- In the employment provisions of the SDA sexual harassment is seen as a form of sex discrimination and it is possible that a pupil complaining of sexual harassment by a teacher or another pupil could pursue a civil law claim against the school under the education provisions of the Act

Issues to be considered

- Is a school able to target particular activities at either boys or girls, in their best interests, without unlawfully excluding the other sex?

- Are single-sex schools offering the full range of options, work experience opportunities, and vocational courses which pupils would encounter in a comparable mixed school?

- Are there any problems for schools in establishing rules regarding clothes, jewellery, and hair length and style, which result in less favourable treatment for one sex than the other? How can these be overcome?

What Schools can do

- LEAs and schools can ensure that a common test is used when selecting pupils for admission, that the test scores are calculated without the use of any sex norms, and that the same pass mark is used for both sexes. Furthermore, when selecting pupils the school should avoid using any procedures which place an undue or unnecessary emphasis on specific skills which might, because of traditional expectations and cultural stereotyping, put one sex at a disadvantage.

- Schools can make efforts to use setting criteria which do not disadvantage either sex. Where possible they should try to ensure that all aspects of a pupil's work in a subject are taken into account when allocating pupils to sets. A pupil's sex should be disregarded when selecting pupils for an over-subscribed class.

- Single-sex schools which do not have facilities to teach the full range of subjects, and might therefore be in breach of the SDA, should discuss their difficulties with the LEA or the Funding Agency for Schools. In some cases it may be appropriate for some sharing of facilities between schools.

Standards of Achievement

- Girls out-perform boys at ages 7, 11, and 14 in National Curriculum assessments in English. Achievements in mathematics and science are broadly similar.

- Girls are more successful than boys at every level in the GCSE:
    - more achieve at least one grade G or above
    - more achieve at least 5 grades G or above
    - more achieve at least one grade C or above
    - more achieve at least 5 grades C or above - more achieve grade A*.

- Girls are more successful than boys (in terms of achieving GCSE grades A* to C), or broadly as successful, in almost all major subjects. They are even achieving success in subjects traditionally considered "boys' subjects" (design and technology, computer studies, mathematics, chemistry, and combined science), though their performance is usually relatively less good in these subjects than in others.

- The only major subject in which girls perform significantly less well than boys is GCSE physics. Similarly, their performance was relatively weak in the physical processes element of National Curriculum science when assessed at age 14 in 1992.

- At A-level and AS (Advanced Supplementary) boys gain very low or very high point scores more often than girls. For any given level of GCSE score, the female candidates appear to be less likely to achieve high A-level or AS scores than male candidates. This is more marked amongst candidates with high GCSE scores. For example, amongst candidates with total GCSE points scores of 60 or more in 1992, 32% of male candidates and 22% of female candidates achieved A-level or AS scores of 30 or more in 1994.

- The pattern of differences in the performance of the sexes in the various subjects at GCSE is not continued at A-level.

Trends

- The gap between girls' and boys' achievement at GCSE has been roughly the same for several years. There are statistical difficulties in making comparisons with the previous years, but it is possible that the difference is greater than it was when GCSE was first taken in 1988.

- There are also statistical difficulties in analysing the O-level and CSE results of the 1980s, but they appear to show that girls were already improving their performance before GCSE was introduced. The EOC's research report *Education Reforms and Gender Equality in Schools* presents a detailed comparative study of examination entry and performance data for 1984-94.

- The changes to GCSE criteria affecting the 1994 results, including the reduction of the coursework element, did not immediately reduce the superiority of the girls' performance.

Issues to be considered

- Did girls perform increasingly better in the first years of GCSE because they took to this new form of examination more readily than boys? If so, why has their lead steadied rather than reduced?

- The O-level and CSE courses of the 1980s did not always make use of coursework, whereas this has been a strong feature of most GCSE courses. Should we attribute girls' better achievement at GCSE to its use of coursework? If so, why have girls been more able than boys to take advantage of this element? Moreover, if this was a factor why did girls' superiority not diminish following the recent changes in GCSE criteria?

- Is the levelling up of the sexes in the sixth form accounted for by boys having caught up with girls in intellectual maturity?

- Is it related to the more selective nature of sixth form provision, and the under-representation there of the less academically successful? Why, if so, should this affect the performance of boys more than girls?

- Do the styles of examining - or of teaching - in the sixth form vary from those at Key Stages 1 to 4 in ways which benefit the boys and disadvantage the girls?

- Why do boys do better than girls in A-level General Studies? This course differs from many in that it covers a broad range of curricular areas, and preparation for the examination tends to focus less on revision of specific skills and knowledge than in many subjects.

- Are there other factors, either within the control of the educational system or not, which lead one sex to out-perform the other? Some are discussed in the following sections on Effective Schools and The Quality of Learning.

What Schools can do

- Clusters of schools can work together to identify local or regional characteristics in the profile of achievement by both sexes. They can then work with local communities, TECs (Training and Enterprise Councils), and employers to raise expectations if one sex is under-performing. Equality targets can be developed, taking account of local circumstances, to focus on raising the achievement of the under performing group, either in an area of the curriculum or in terms of a more general educational target such as post-16 participation. This could then lead to a sharing of strategies between schools and a joint evaluation of progress.

- Governors and headteachers can monitor the standards achieved in each area of the curriculum in order to identify patterns of different achievement by girls and boys. They can attempt to identify factors leading to changes from year to year, and trace trends over several years. IT-assisted analysis is a beneficial tool which secondary schools can use.

- Senior managers can then target particular initiatives to suit the school's needs. In an effort to combat under-achievement some schools are currently implementing measures to boost the achievement of boys in English, or girls in physics, or are introducing specifically targeted extra-curricular activities. Some schools, including primaries, have introduced projects to improve pupils' self-esteem in order that pupils can develop higher aspirations. Others are developing tight monitoring procedures at Key Stage 4 to ensure that pupils meet GCSE coursework requirements and introducing some mentoring of pupils who need particular guidance. Certain schools, using LEA support, are trying to measure the value added to each sex's performance as pupils progress through the key stages in order to provide support, whether curricular or tutorial, where it is most needed. As yet there has been little systematic evaluation of initiatives such as these, but individual schools are reporting some successes.

Effective Schools

Inspection Evidence

An effective school is one where pupils' achievement is all that might reasonably be expected given the composition of its intake, and where the quality of education provided meets the needs of all groups within the pupil population. In an effective school, girls and boys would make broadly similar progress in relation to their capabilities. The curriculum, both formal and hidden, would prepare them equally and fully for their lives as adult citizens. Inspectors evaluate the extent to which a school understands and meets the needs of both sexes and helps all pupils to develop their talents to the full.

● OFSTED inspections show that almost all schools are reasonably effective in the most fundamental aspect of providing equal opportunities: they meet relevant legislative requirements and do not explicitly discriminate against either sex in making curricular provision.

● The inspections also show that nearly half of primary schools and one third of middle schools, all of these being mixed schools, achieve considerable success in more generally meeting gender needs, although only one fifth of mixed secondary schools are as successful. In these schools, both sexes contribute well to lessons and achieve to their potential, and pupils are prepared realistically for adult life in a diverse society. Some single-sex schools, especially girls' schools, also meet their pupils' needs very well by helping pupils to develop broad horizons and by promoting high expectations across a range of educational targets. These successful schools, whether mixed or single-sex, usually have headteachers with a strong commitment to developing equality of opportunity, and a system of self-evaluation which gives attention to gender issues. They have normally involved staff in developing relevant policies through which they have identified issues for action, sometimes with the involvement of governors. Action taken in various of these schools has included modifying some PE activities to enable both sexes to be involved on equal terms, implementing measures to deal with sexual harassment, and initiating staff development strategies to support all newly-promoted staff.

- Schools which successfully meet gender needs tend to be successful in other fundamental aspects. They are likely to have good standards across the curriculum, to be harmonious working communities, and to have developed good partnership with parents. It seems that effective schools often have equal opportunities at the heart of their agendas because their proper concern for the individual is illuminated by an understanding of how a young person's educational choices and achievements can be influenced by their gender. At best, these schools take an explicit approach to equal opportunities which is based on consideration of relevant evidence. However, merely giving prominence to an equal opportunities policy does not guarantee that both sexes are well provided for; that is only achieved through rigorous monitoring of the policy at all levels and by striving towards a more general effectiveness.

- About one secondary school in five is weak in meeting the particular needs of one or the other sex. In these, some or all of the following characteristics obtain: one sex might be seriously under-performing in lessons or in examinations; the books and resources used might not take appropriate account of gender issues; pupils might not be being prepared well for opportunities in working life.

- Some inspection evidence suggests that the circumstances and levels of effectiveness of schools might affect girls and boys in different ways. It appears that the differences in performance between girls and boys in mixed schools are greater in successful schools than other schools. Successful schools are efficiently managed schools which achieve good standards overall, provide effective teaching in an orderly environment and are concerned for the progress and development of the individual pupils. Where these conditions do not apply, girls' performance tends to decline more than boys'.

- Girls' schools tend to cater more positively for equal opportunities than boys' schools. They often have a longer history of considering gender issues, in particular of building into their curriculum an awareness of the significance of gender as a factor in the world of work. This is discussed in greater detail in the section later in this paper on Single-sex and Mixed Schools.

Issues to be considered

- In 1992 an HMI survey, *The Preparation of Girls for Adult and Working Life* (published by the then Department of Education and Science) found that "In mixed schools, generalised statements about boys and girls as pupils had an egalitarian flavour which in some places had the unfortunate consequence of disguising the specific needs of adolescent boys and adolescent girls." Is the suggestion that schools should consider the specific needs of each sex within their overall policy-making appropriate only to older pupils, or does it apply equally to primary schools?

- How can schools resolve the issues of equity raised in any attempt to meet the needs of one sex more effectively by taking some form of positive action? Will assisting one sex distract from the needs of the other, or even possibly disadvantage the other? Or will it lead to an enhanced awareness of gender which will ultimately be to the advantage of all pupils?

- Should schools plan action specifically to meet gender needs, or will general action to promote effectiveness automatically bring with it improvements in equality of opportunity?

- Is the frequent failure of secondary schools to achieve the same success with boys as they achieve with girls related to any failures schools might have in building rapport with boys?

What Schools can do

- Schools can make progress in promoting equal opportunities by developing a clear policy covering all aspects of the institution's work. Staff teams can be required to reflect this policy in their detailed planning and action plans can define specific targets. A senior member of staff can monitor and evaluate implementation of the policy and report to the governing body on the levels of effectiveness reached.

The Curriculum

Evidence

- Boys and girls following the National Curriculum now take largely the same courses aged from 5 to 14. The main exception is in physical education, where boys tend to have a narrower curriculum than girls in Key Stage 3, with more limited opportunities for dance or gymnastics.

- Boys and girls in mixed schools generally have, in formal terms, equal access to the same extra-curricular activities, though the pattern of their involvement is often gender-related: for instance, boys are frequently under-represented in musical activities; in extra-curricular PE or sports activities at secondary level, boys outnumber girls at least 2 to 1.

- When subject options are introduced beyond the National Curriculum at Key Stage 4, pupils sometimes make their choices on traditional lines, reflecting stereotyped views of what is appropriate for their gender. Broadly speaking, scientific and technical subjects attract more boys; languages and arts attract more girls.

- However, more girls are now taking the traditional boys' subjects (such as design and technology), although boys are still reluctant to take the traditional girls' subjects such as home economics.

- Subject choices in the sixth form, reflecting students' individual preferences and perceived needs, are sometimes heavily influenced by gender: boys favouring physics, economics, mathematics, chemistry and geography, with girls favouring sociology, French, English Literature, biology, and art and design.

- The most troubling aspect of the gender pattern of sixth form study is that, despite their success in these subjects at GCSE, relatively few young women are taking A-level courses which are wholly mathematical, scientific or technological, thereby denying themselves some career opportunities in science, engineering and technology.

- About half of secondary schools have initiatives under way intended to broaden pupils' thinking about subject choices and careers. These sometimes make good use of outside agencies and they build well on work experience programmes. Nevertheless, progress is very slow. Few schools, primary or secondary, have developed a co-ordinated approach which aims to educate pupils about gender.

- During the 1980s, many single-sex schools improved their accommodation so that they could teach the full range of technology. However, although most girls' schools now have facilities for work with resistant materials and in control technology, a large number of boys' schools still have inadequate facilities for work in textiles or in food technology and may therefore provide narrower opportunities than local mixed schools.

Issues to be considered

- How can schools encourage more girls to prepare for careers in science, engineering and technology?

- To what extent should schools seek to influence the preferences of pupils choosing optional courses? Do schools feel it is their responsibility to try to encourage pupils into areas of the curriculum which are not traditional for their sex?

- In view of the concerns sometimes expressed currently about young adults' skills in parenthood, and given the need to educate both sexes for parenthood and family life, is there a case for secondary schools running courses in child development for all pupils?

- In some secondary schools, a commitment to mixed physical education can restrict pupils' achievement. In some primaries, however, pupils are grouped by sex for certain physical education activities without there being any clear benefit. Are there certain principles schools can use to guide decisions about the appropriateness of mixed or single-sex groupings?

What Schools can do

- Schools should evaluate the curriculum they provide in order to judge whether it meets their declared aims and whether it prepares all pupils equally for adult and working life. They need to monitor their use of the discretionary time available to them once statutory requirements have been met.

- Senior managers and subject leaders should monitor the patterns of recruitment of optional subjects, and of options within subjects such as technology. They also need to monitor vocational courses to ascertain the patterns of recruitment to the various career fields.

- Schools can consider a variety of measures which might promote the involvement of girls in scientific and technical courses after age 16. These might include reviewing the curriculum offered in these subjects, making greater use of outside agencies to demonstrate the applicability of the subjects, introducing relevant extra-curricular activities, and mentoring individual pupils, as these methods have brought some success in similar fields.

- Similarly, schools can use special means to promote the take-up of extra-curricular activities by one sex or the other. Some schools have introduced single-sex, extra-curricular groups for certain activities to give the less dominant sex an opportunity to gain initial confidence in a relatively sheltered situation. Successes are reported but there is a need for further analysis.

- Some useful curriculum developments aimed at promoting equality of opportunity were developed through the Technical and Vocational Education Initiative (TVEI) in the 1980s and early 1990s. Some schools made progress in attracting young people to non-traditional subjects by examining curriculum structures. This could include broadening provision in subjects such as craft design technology and home economics, reducing early choices, scrutinising the pattern of option blocks offered and improving guidance to pupils. There are lessons here still to be learned in other schools.

The Quality of Learning

- There is considerable research and inspection evidence to suggest that, although an individual's attitude to learning is clearly not predetermined by their gender, there are tendencies for girls and boys to respond in certain general ways in given circumstances. OFSTED's forthcoming review of research findings will analyse this in detail, but the following section outlines some key areas as a preliminary.

Evidence

- An HMI survey of *Girls Learning Mathematics* (1989) showed that girls tend to underestimate their abilities in the subject and to be discouraged by adverse circumstances. They are most successful when the teaching gives them a chance to talk ideas through and place mathematical concepts in a relevant context.

- An HMI inspection of *Boys and English* (1993) pointed out that secondary age boys tend to have more negative attitudes towards reading and writing than girls. They often have narrower experiences of fiction, write more predictably, and have difficulty with the affective aspects of English. Their learning improves when the teaching convinces them of the value of what they are doing, and gives them a clearer understanding of the variety of language use. The use of information technology can benefit the quality of their work.

- Some research evidence, supported by inspection findings, suggests that girls tend to lack confidence in using the concepts of physical science in their technology work, even when their competence is equivalent to that of boys. Their capability in designing and making, often initially less strong than boys' in the early years - perhaps because of differences in experiences in play - can be boosted by focused teaching initiatives; but this does not so easily lead to an increase in confidence. Their designs can therefore lack innovation and vigour.

- National Curriculum assessments suggest that girls are more successful than boys in some of the more reflective aspects of work: in applying mathematics; in having ideas for using technology; and in assessing the results of technological projects.

- Boys' and girls' recreational experiences often lead to them developing certain physical skills from an early age. Girls are more frequently involved in gymnastics and dance outside school, whilst boys are more likely to have experience of invasive games, such as football. Not surprisingly, inspection suggests that this affects the prowess they show in aspects of the PE curriculum.

- Inspectors often note that girls and boys have different approaches to planning and organising their work. Girls are more likely to remember to bring the right equipment to lessons and to complete their homework diaries. They are more likely to respond to teachers' comments on their work. These differences, however, become less apparent among high achieving pupils.

- Lesson observation indicates that in some subjects, such as technology, girls can work below their potential by maintaining a high level of activity but in fairly low level tasks. This, together with girls' generally good management of their work, can mislead teachers into thinking these girls are making progress.

Issues to be considered

- To what extent are pupils' attitudes to learning, their confidence in particular subjects, and their eventual success affected by their gender? Is it possible to establish meaningful generalisations without constructing stereotypes?

- How do pupils' gender-related attitudes change as they mature and why are some pupils more influenced by their gender than others? Why do some pupils put barriers to progress in front of themselves? What role is played by social class, culture and geographic location?

- It appears that one reason why girls often achieve more than boys in school is that they more often demonstrate diligence, good behaviour and enthusiasm for learning. If this is so, how can schools encourage boys to acquire these qualities?

- Should pre-school provision take more account of the influence which pupils' early experience of play and social relationships has in shaping their notion of what is appropriate for their gender?

- Is it possible that the under-performance of some secondary age boys in French relates to difficulty they may have in producing good spoken language? Do they feel more awkward than most girls in pronouncing some of the French vowel sounds, and in mastering the intonation, and does such awkwardness restrict their confidence in the language? Is this less true of other modern foreign languages, such as German or Spanish?

What Schools can do

- Schools can analyse pupils' involvement in learning activities in the early years and identify any emerging gender-related patterns, in order to intervene to extend pupils' experiences. For instance, schools can introduce specific initiatives in nursery and Key Stage 1 classes targeting girls who lack experience in constructional activity. Equally, teachers can ensure that boys' prowess in gymnastics is promoted by the use of demonstrations by the more talented boys.

- Subject co-ordinators and heads of department can draw on research findings and inspection evidence in implementing initiatives to boost the confidence and achievement of either sex where there are weaknesses.

- Schools can encourage boys to understand that good management of their work is part of the learning task. They can teach boys to maintain their written work coherently and usably, and to meet deadlines. Equally, they can dissuade any girls who are over-concerned with the presentation of their work from devoting time to this aspect at the expense of others.

- Schools can consider how they promote teachers' awareness of the different needs of boys and girls, and pupils' understanding of each others' points of view. Where governors and senior managers feel that gender is a factor influencing pupils' progress they can analyse the extent to which the school helps pupils to think about gender as an aspect of their identity in order that it should not determine their post-school destinations.

Personal and Social Development

Girls mature physically more rapidly than boys and this is usually mirrored in their personal and social behaviour. Different rates of maturation have implications for achievement and learning, and also for how schools approach personal and social development.

Evidence

- An HMI survey, *Homework in Primary and Secondary Schools* (1995) showed that girls tend to predominate amongst those older primary pupils who spend more than an average time on homework projects; this, it was suggested, results from a desire to achieve high standards or to please their teachers.

- Inspectors frequently find that boys and girls choose to work and play separately. They seldom opt to do collaborative or group work in mixed sex groups, and sometimes show a marked reluctance to do so. Some teachers deliberately organise some mixed group working to broaden pupils' perspectives and experiences, though the outcomes appear to be variable. Inspection evidence suggests that teachers need to have very clear objectives for such work and have to organise the groups' work carefully if it is to be successful.

- Most pupils behave well, but schools find the behaviour of a small minority of boys difficult to manage: boys are four times as likely to be excluded from school as girls, often because of aggressive behaviour.

- There is little inspection evidence to determine the prevalence of sexual harassment in schools; however, there are some examples of girls being subjected to verbal harassment or inappropriate touching by boys. The EOC receives a small number of complaints which indicate the existence but not the extent of the problem. Some schools have established clear codes of conduct which outlaw such behaviour.

- Many secondary schools use personal and social education (PSE) courses as a means to raise pupils' understanding of gender, personal relationships, and related social concerns. However, an HMI survey,

Personal and Social Education in some Secondary Schools (1988) found that within PSE courses in general, there was little sign of potentially controversial aspects of work being explored in sufficient detail; more attention often needed to be given to evidence in discussion, and to the underlying moral dilemmas. More recent inspection evidence tends to support this finding.

● HMI's survey, *The Preparation of Girls for Adult and Working Life* (1992) also found that in mixed secondary schools men tended to predominate in governing bodies and in the senior levels of school staffing structures. It is not possible to calculate what effect, if any, this has on pupils' emerging understanding of adult roles in society, but the HMI report pointed out that "coherent approaches to equal opportunities would be helped by representation of women and men on teaching staffs and governing bodies to reflect views and experiences present in wider society".

● Primary school pupils are likely to see women or mothers providing general classroom support and men or fathers coming into lessons to talk about their jobs. This may have the effect of influencing pupils' notions about adult roles and the world of work. Many schools, however, now try to ensure a gender balance amongst visiting speakers.

Issues to be considered

● What steps should schools take to identify and eliminate sexual harassment? How serious is this problem? Are boys always the aggressors?

● Does the over-representation of boys amongst pupils excluded from school imply that boys are being unfairly discriminated against in the application of sanctions?

● Should mixed schools combat the narrowing of experience which can derive from some pupils choosing to work and play mainly in single-sex groupings?

● Are some boys subject to peer group or parental pressures which militate against educational achievement? Do some boys feel they have less investment in education than girls? Is this more evident in some areas and social groupings than in others? Does it apply more in mixed schools than single-sex schools? If these pressures exist, what can schools do to make these boys more relaxed about being seen to be keen to study and to achieve academically?

- It is sometimes argued that the educational system intrinsically favours girls because it puts a premium on those aspects of the personality in which girls at present show themselves to be strong, such as self-management of work and personal application. If this is accurate, how can schools ensure that boys are not disadvantaged? Can schools make greater use of aspects in which many boys are strong, such as competitiveness, in order to maximise their achievements?

- While girls are now achieving better academic results than boys at age 16, there is little evidence to indicate that this is leading to improved post-school opportunities in the form of training, employment, career development and economic independence for the majority of young women. Are schools focusing on the academic achievement of girls, and neglecting the important and complementary skills of individual development and decision making which enable young people to maximise their opportunities later on? How can schools challenge traditional expectations and roles in order to improve pupils' aspirations and strengthen their life choices and chances?

- Girls often appear to be more open and willing to exchange ideas, and to be good listeners. In an attempt to develop both sexes, some mixed schools have occasionally provided single-sex classes within PSE, whilst others have carefully engineered small group discussion which, if well structured, ensures a balance of male and female speaking and listening. Do both girls and boys gain from these experiences?

What Schools can do

- Schools can audit the range of role models to which pupils are exposed at school. They can plan a work experience programme which is consistent with the school's equal opportunities policy. They can arrange work 'shadowing' to ensure that pupils develop an informed understanding of adult roles in society.

- A review of the use of rewards and sanctions may throw light on gender-related behaviour patterns in a school. Evaluation of the school's behaviour policy could take account of the need to motivate all pupils and might suggest steps that could be taken to prevent the development of some poor behaviour.

- Pastoral work could include the enhanced mentoring of individual pupils whose achievement appeared at risk from the adverse effects of peer group pressure. Equally, some schools could make greater use of praise of individuals in order to focus their attention on making progress.

- Each staff team can plan strategies to promote the personal and social development of girls and boys. For instance, Key Stage 2 teachers might implement a programme to improve some boys' attitudes to homework, perhaps providing more short term targets and some tutorial support. Key Stage 3 teachers might seek to promote girls' assertiveness if there were evidence that they were victims of sexual harassment.

- Many schools already create opportunities for pupils of both sexes to gain experience in serving their peers by taking on regular class routines, or in representing others through election to a school committee or council. This can play an important part in extending pupils' empathetic understanding and their ability to see beyond gender-related concerns.

Single-sex and Mixed Schools

The comparison of single-sex and mixed schools is contentious and very complex; there is no straightforward answer to whether one type of school is more successful than the other because so many variables are involved.

Evidence

- An analysis of inspection reports suggests that the quality of education in single-sex and mixed schools reflects well-established differences in the performance and attitudes of girls and boys. In other words, the fact that girls generally have more positive attitudes than boys, and achieve higher standards, is a significant factor in the relative success of the different types of school. Therefore, in almost all the areas covered by the *Framework for Inspection*, girls' schools are generally found to perform best, mixed schools next, and boys' schools least effectively. There are, however, marked variations in the positions of individual schools, whether mixed or single-sex, within this hierarchy. Much depends on the socio-economic context of the school and the ability profile of its intake.

- Schools in favoured areas consistently receive more favourable judgements from inspectors than schools in disadvantaged areas, with regard to standards, management and efficiency, ethos and the overall quality of education. This can sometimes accentuate the effect of gender: the schools judged to be the most successful are often girls' schools in advantaged areas. Other factors may also affect the quality of schools as judged by inspectors: for instance, both boys' grammar schools and girls' grammar schools tend to be judged more highly than mixed grammar schools. This, however, may be an effect of differences in the ability profiles of the various types of school.

- Most of the single-sex schools are found by inspectors to be improving. Purposeful and effective management, often from newly-appointed headteachers with high expectations of their staff and pupils, is identified in the reports on over half the girls' and boys' schools. Many are working towards carefully thought-out objectives for improvement, and in a few cases the boys' schools even appear to be achieving greater success than adjacent girls' schools with similar intakes. These improvements may account for the findings of a recent statistical analysis undertaken by OFSTED, that girls and boys in single-sex schools now achieve slightly better GCSE results than girls and boys in mixed schools, after account has been taken of available socio-economic data including free school meal entitlement.

- Nevertheless, even if boys' comprehensives and boys' grammar schools are in some respects competing effectively with their mixed counterparts, this may not be the result of their single-sex status. Research studies in the past into girls' schools have tended to indicate that it may be a function of other factors such as parental support, social class and the attainment of pupils on entry to the school.

- There are relatively few single-sex schools in England, and they often have distinctive features which may indicate a particular commitment by parents (see Table). A high proportion of single-sex schools are selective. The proportion of pupils from ethnic minority groups, and in particular from ethnic minority families with high educational aspirations, may well be higher in single-sex than mixed schools. Single-sex schools, especially girls' schools, are often fully subscribed or over-subscribed, which can indicate high levels of parental support, and may have implications for academic and educational success. There is some evidence that in many single-sex schools pupils may have travelled from a considerable distance, further indicating the committment of the parents who select these schools. This may be because of the perceived success of the school or because of other factors: single-sex schools are slightly more likely than mixed schools to be voluntary aided and to have religious affiliations. Overall, therefore, even though some single-sex schools may have high rates of entitlement to free school meals, this may not necessarily represent the attitudes and aspirations that are sometimes associated with disadvantage.

- Numerous uncertainties need to be taken into account in considering the respective merits of mixed and single-sex schools in achieving high standards. Further research and inspection evidence will be needed before secure conclusions can be drawn.

Issues to be considered

- The inspection evidence tends to suggest that girls' schools in average and disadvantaged areas, and boys' schools more generally, do relatively little to try to broaden pupils' horizons beyond traditional and often stereotypical expectations. Furthermore, the inspection reports do not show clearly that boys and girls in single-sex schools always receive better provision in subjects which are non-traditional for their sex than do their peers in mixed schools, although they may be more likely to choose non-traditional subjects in the sixth form. Are there ways of ensuring that single-sex schools use their status as single-sex schools more effectively? For instance, are there ways in which boys' schools can make a unique contribution to the education of boys in a society where expectations of men appear to be changing rapidly?

- Are there ways of replicating in mixed schools certain identifiable benefits of single-sex education? Should mixed schools experiment more with single-sex grouping for specific purposes, or would this be expensive and difficult to justify?

What Schools can do

- Boys' schools should pay particular attention to the general under-achievement of boys in word-centred subjects, and to boys' perceptions of themselves, their future roles in life, and the skills they will need if they are to fulfil their potential. Under-achievement should be discussed openly with boys and their parents, and the implications made clear of society's increasing reliance on communication skills.

- Girls' schools should be wary of the complacency which might result from the current attention to the high performance of girls. They need to analyse the achievements of girls across subjects, identify where most and least value is added, look at the girls' selection of subjects and future destinations, and plan ways of raising standards and aspirations further and counteracting any residual stereotypical attitudes.

TABLE SHOWING THE NUMBER OF SINGLE-SEX AND MIXED SCHOOLS IN ENGLAND

Number of Primary Schools (including middle deemed primary)

Mixed		18,547
Single-sex		4
boys	2	
girls	2	
Total		**18,551**

Number of Secondary Schools (including middle deemed secondary)

Mixed		3,190
Single-sex		424
boys	197	
girls	227	
Total		**3,614**

Mixed denominational		485
Single-sex denominational		88
boys	40	
girls	48	
Total		**573**

Mixed voluntary aided		295
Single-sex voluntary aided		58
boys	27	
girls	31	
Total		**353**

Mixed comprehensive		2,592
Single-sex comprehensive		265
boys	118	
girls	147	
Total		**2,857**
Mixed selective		41
Single-sex selective		116
boys	56	
girls	60	
Total		**157**
Mixed sec. modern		112
Single-sex secondary modern		29
boys	14	
girls	15	
Total		**141**

Source DfEE School Census (Form 7) 1995

Responses

This publication has been produced by OFSTED and the EOC to encourage and inform debate. Readers are invited to respond by commenting on the general ideas expressed or on particular evidence highlighted or initiatives noted. OFSTED and the EOC would also welcome responses which drew attention to areas of evidence **not** referred to in the paper.

If possible, responses should be sent to:

Oona Stannard, HMI
OFSTED
Alexandra House
33 Kingsway
London WC2B 6SE

and to:

Anne Madden
Education and Training Unit
Equal Opportunities Commission
Overseas House
Quay Street Manchester M3 3HN

Bibliography

HMI and OFSTED Publications

Boys and Modern Languages (1985)
HMI55/85 Department for Education and Science (Pub. Centre)

Girls and Science (1980)
HMSO ISBN 0 11 270534 0 £3.30 (Out of print)

A Survey of Personal and Social Education Courses in Some Secondary Schools (1988)
Department of Education and Science HMI report 88/235 (Out of print

Education Observed No. 14: Girls Learning Mathematics (1989)
Department of Education and Science ISBN 0855222182 (Out of print)

The Preparation of Girls for Adult and Working Life (1992)
Department for Education HMI Report 209/92 (Out of Print)

Boys and English (1993)
HMR 002/93/NS OFSTED (Pub. Centre)

Science and Mathematics in Schools - A Review (1994)
HMSO ISBN 0 11 350044 0 £6.50

Physical Education and Sport in Schools: a Survey of Good Practice (1996) HMSO ISBN 0 11 350075 0 £4.50

Assessing School Effectiveness: Developing Measures to put School Performance in Context: a report by the Institute of Education for the Office for Standards in Education (1994) OFSTED (Pub. Centre)

Homework in Primary and Secondary Schools (1995)
HMSO ISBN 0 11 350064 5 £3.95

Framework for the Inspection of Schools (1995)
OFSTED HMI74 (Pub. Centre)

HMSO Publications can be ordered from the HMSO Orderline on: 0171-873 9090.

OFSTED HMI Publications are available from the OFSTED Publications Centre and are free of charge.
They can be ordered by telephoning 0171-510 0180.

EOC Publications

The Life Cycle of Inequality: Women and Men in Britain (1995)
ISBN:1 870 358457 £12.95

Sex Discrimination in Schools - A Guide for Governors on the Elimination of Sex Discrimination and the Promotion of Equal Opportunities in Schools (revised 1991) ISBN: 870358 09 9 £1.50

An Equal Start - Guidelines on Equal Treatment for the Under-Eights (revised 1994) ISBN: 1870358 13 9 £3.00

West Glamorgan Schools: access to craft subjects in School Curricula in Primary and Secondary Schools (1994) £0.50

Positive Action in Vocational Education and Training: section 47 of the Sex Discrimination Act (1994) £0.50

Educational Reforms and Gender Equality in Schools,
by M. Arnot, M. David and G. Weiner (1996) Research Discussion Series No. 17 ISBN: 1870358 54 6 £14.95

Inquiry into Education and Training for 14-19 Year-Olds (October 1995) EOC Submission to the House of Commons' Select Committee on Education

Response of the EOC to the National Advisory Council for Education and Training Consultation (NACETT) (October 1994)

EOC Publications are available from:

Publications Unit
Equal Opportunities Commission
Overseas House
Quay Street
Manchester M3 3HN
Tel: 0161-833 9244
Fax: 0161-835 1657

Other publications

The Rising Tide: A Report on Women in Science, Engineering and Technology (1994) produced by the Committee on Women in Science, Engineering and Technology HMSO ISBN 0 11 430096 8 £7.50

Women in Science, Engineering and Technology; a Government Response to the Report: The Rising Tide (July 1994)
ISBN 0 11 430103 4 £3.95

Differential Performance of Boys and Girls in Examinations at 16+: English and Mathematics Final report by ULEAC and NFER for SEAC (1992)

Language Performance in Schools: 1982 Secondary Report Assessment of Performance Unit HMSO (1988) ISBN 0 11 270620 7 (Out of print)

Gender Differences and GCSE results Centre for Successful Schools; Keele University (1994)

Changing Lives Nos. 1-3 by Catherine Shaw, Policy Studies Institute (1994) No.1 ISBN 088 5374 6257; No 2 ISBN 088 5374 626 5; No. 3 ISBN 088 5374 641 9

A Fair Test? - Assessment, Achievement and Equity by C. Gipps and P. Murphy (1994) OU Press ISBN 0335156738 £15.99

Gender and Education (Journal)
Department of Continuing Education, University of Warwick
Subscriptions available from Carfax Publishers, P O Box 25, Abingdon, Oxfordshire OX14 3UE

Young People in 1994: The Health Related Behaviour Questionnaire Results (1995) John Balding; University of Exeter; Schools Health Education Unit, Heavitree Road, Exeter, EX1 2LU Tel: 01392 264722 ISBN 85068 160X

Gender, Primary Schools and the National Curriculum (1992) NASUWT and the Engineering Council A Smithies and P Zientek £5.50

Job Ambitions of the Next Generation: a Survey of Careers Aspirations of Teenagers and their Parents (1995)
MORI Survey; City and Guilds Institute

Equal Opportunities in Modern Apprenticeships: Lessons from the Prototypes (1995); Final report by R. Travers and A. Magill DfEE

Genderwatch: After the Education Reform Act (1992)
devised and edited by K. Myers; Cambridge University Press,
ISBN: 0521 407826

Equality of Opportunity in the Classroom
Coventry Education Department (1993) Available from Elm Bank
Teachers' Centre, Mile Lane, Coventry, CV1 2LQ

Exploring Equal Opportunities (1995) £65
by G. Hughes and W. Smith, Daniels Publishing ISBN 1854672045

When I Grow Up I Want To Be...
(A Primary Curriculum Resource Pack produced by the London
Borough of Waltham Forest Careers Service;) COIC (1992)

Challenging Choices: Final Project Report
Somerset Education Services (1994) (Available from the County Equal
Opportunities Officer).